Decisions

Antoyne L. Green

Eleos Press

Rogersville, Alabama

First Edition

However God Chooses

Author: Antoyne L. Green
© 2014 by Antoyne L. Green

All rights reserved.

This book or parts thereof may not be reproduced in any form, stored in a retrieval system, or transmitted in any form by any means without prior written permission of the author, except as provided by United States of America copyright law.

Cover Design: Eleos Press
Interior Formatting: Eleos Press

www.eleospress.com

Also available in eBook form

ISBN-13: 978-0692257340

PRINTED IN THE UNITED STATES OF AMERICA

INTRODUCTION

It's very likely that you've made quite a few of them today. Some were easy. Others weren't. You thought little about a few of them. Others required some careful pondering and maybe even prayer. Decisions. They affect what we do, how we do it, and when we do it. Decisions. They often serve in the same capacity as the throttle lever on a lawn mower. Based on what we decide about something, the decision can thrust actions and reactions from us into "fast" mode or throttle us down into slow motion. Decisions. Often they're like psychological remote controls. They push our emotional buttons to the degree that we'll be extremely happy, sorely sorrowful, or somewhere in between based on what we decide about a person, a particular issue, or plans for our lives.

Certainly, all decisions aren't that deep. What shirt do I wear today? Sandals or sneakers? Biscuits or bagels? Movies or dinner? Sleep in or get up early and knock out some work? However, decisions can be very intense when they will deeply and drastically affect our lives and/or the lives of those we love dearly. Just ask Jochebed—Moses' mother. This loving mother made some awfully tough decisions when it came to her baby boy. Within the pages of this book, it's very likely that you'll feel Jochebed's emotions and conflicts within as she arrived at some very tough crossroads. What do you do when it's time to make a decision and what your ***head*** desires and what your ***heart*** determines as best are two different things? What do you do when the ***right*** thing to do feels so ***wrong*** deep down inside? What do you do when what you're ***comfortable*** deciding doesn't match what God is ***compelling*** you to decide? These are the unenviable places that we've all found ourselves in before. That's why I'm confident Jochebed's plight will become very personal to you as you continue to read.

Learn from this caring woman that a firm faith in God when it comes to making hard decisions touches the heart of God. Learn from Jochebed that joy will follow making the right, God-led decision—even though it may be heartbreaking at the time you're making it. Learn from Moses' mom that God provides for us and favors us after making Spirit-led decisions—*if* we wait patiently on Him. Jochebed will teach us that in all decisions, the ONLY real decision is to trust God IN all things and FOR all things. C'mon, friend. Let's visit Jochebed and Moses.

TABLE OF CONTENTS

INTRODUCTION I

ONE—THE ENEMY ALREADY KNOWS 1

TWO—PRODUCTIVE UNDER PRESSURE 15

THREE—TRAIN YOUNG CHAMPIONS 27

FOUR—FEAR PRODUCES FAVOR OF GOD 37

FIVE—THE BEAUTIFUL BLESSING 49

SIX—THE STRUGGLE WITHIN 59

SEVEN—HE [SHE] WON'T DROWN 71

EIGHT—KEPT 83

NINE—COVERED 95

TEN—WATCHED 109

ELEVEN—RESCUED 119

TWELVE—IT WAS A DIVINE SET-UP 133

THIRTEEN—JUST DO WHAT YOU DO 147

ONE

THE ENEMY ALREADY KNOWS

"He told his people, 'These Israelites are becoming a threat to us because there are so many of them. [10] We must find a way to put an end to this. If we don't and if war breaks out, they will join our enemies and fight against us. Then they will escape from the country." **Exodus 1:9-10 NLT**

Slavery. Bondage. Oppression. If one were to open a dictionary and locate these three words, a picture of an Israelite slave while in

Egypt would certainly be appropriate to define and describe the words. Cruel. Ruthless. Insensitive. Beside these three words in a dictionary, a picture of an Egyptian taskmaster would certainly fit. The Egyptians and their new king, Pharaoh, certainly had the nation of Israel on lockdown. For so long the Egyptians reigned supreme over the Israelites. In fact, a quick read of the Exodus 1 lets us know that *at the moment* the Egyptians were still very much in control. However, the text suggests that Pharaoh began seeing and sensing something different about the Hebrew slaves he was holding hostage. He's getting leery. His nerves of steel are softening. He thinks. Then he continues to observe Israel. In Exodus 1:7 we're told that Israel *"multiplied so quickly that they soon filled the land."* Pharaoh keeps thinking. Then he speaks to the Egyptians—and may I contemporize it—*"Ya'll,*

Decisions

there are a lot of these Israelites here. In fact, there are too many of them. Every day they are having babies. If we don't watch it, they'll outnumber us, overthrow us, and then escape from us." In other words, Pharaoh—Israel's enemy—came to realize that the atmosphere was shifting and eventually Israel's breakthrough from bondage would take place. Pharaoh *already knew* that he wasn't going to be able to hold God's people down very long. The king *already knew* that his victims were bound to be victorious. He *already knew* that his slaves were working their way to being free. Pharaoh *already knew* that those whom he oppressed possessed the ability to overcome.

Let me start early in this book and speak a word of encouragement, empowerment, and enlightenment to you. Satan, our enemy, has strategically planned to oppress you. Sometimes he does it through direct attacks on your finances, your family, your faith, your health, your job status, and in other areas of your life. The enemy uses every available weapon in his arsenal to affect us. Sometimes he infiltrates our minds to shift us to a degree of negativity where we press pause on pursuing so many great things that God has in store for us. Sometimes he uses other people to fluster and frustrate us. Then other times he'll orchestrate situation after situation and issue after issue to disappoint and even devastate us. All of his attacks have one ultimate purpose—to enslave us so he can rule us! Satan wants (and unfortunately has gotten at times) our minds so we won't think like Christ. He wants to dim our focus on our future so we'll hope no more, believe no more, and try no more. He wants to rule our mouths so we'll speak death, destruction, pity, & poverty over

Decisions

our lives and the lives of others instead of speaking life, health, success, and prosperity. Satan wants to rule EVERYTHING. He wants to rule our relationships so they'll be so horrid that we'll fail in them. Furthermore, Satan wants our messed up relationships to be public so some messy people will have something to gossip about and others will shy away from the blessedness of a God-ordained relationship. He wants to rule our finances so we'll stay the debtor and be perpetually broke—or at least with no financial freedom. He wants to control our emotions. He wants to affect our overall being—spiritually, mentally, emotionally, and physically. The devil wants us to be like a radio controlled car. He wants to hold your life's and my life's "remote control." By the flip of his "joystick" he wants to control your every move. I remember my son Kaleb had this remote controlled car that the operator was supposed to intentionally crash it into a wall or another hard surface. Then the car would flip itself over, dash in another direction, and then crash again. Kaleb loved the car and with every crash he laughed louder and louder. Friend, at times we give the enemy the same pleasure. We let our spiritual guards down, lose all the fight we have in us, we just submit and become content with being his slave, and then allow him to control us so we'll crash continually. I can imagine Satan killing himself laughing when we crash in one relationship and then hit a wall in another. He chuckles when we get bent out of shape over something silly on Tuesday and then crash into more nonsense by Friday. He rolls on the floor screaming when we get over one health hurdle and because of bad habits and sometimes sheer neglect of our bodies, we crash again with a

Decisions

different ailment. He bends over slapping his knees in hysteria when we spend outside of our means on the dress, the car, the home, the jewelry, the electronics, the lunches and dinners out, and whatever else that comes to mind. I imagine he then texts a picture of us to his demons while we take weeks to work our way out of our financial holes and then crash again with more idiotic spending. Truth is, we all have times when we either hand the enemy the remote control to our lives or we just tune into his frequency and submit to his control. However, I must encourage you to break the cycle and get ready to live life abundantly, prosperously, and in good health! You CAN do it! You WILL do it because of whose you are! Israel was God's chosen people and the enemy (Pharaoh) knew they couldn't be oppressed forever. Well, you and I are God's chosen folks too! So believe this—our enemy already knows that if we ever get our focus finely tuned on God, any stranglehold he has on us will have to end soon!

Friend, if you read nothing else in the book, please take this one thing to heart: for those of us who have received Jesus as our Savior, we are the children of God. Therefore, we have the _privileges_ of being God's children.

If we focus on our Father, read and study His Word—then live accordingly—we'll align ourselves for deliverance. If we can keep the faith even during times when it _seems_ all hope is lost, then we can and will survive every situation. Understand that the enemy **already knows** that _when_ God stands up in our situation it's a fixed fight! We win! The enemy already knows that when we walk in the power and authority of God we'll trade our fear for a faith that will be

Decisions

rewarded by God's faithfulness. Satan already knows that greater is the power of God _upon_ our lives than his power that comes _against_ our lives. The enemy already knows that after awhile we'll switch positions with him in the spiritual battles we face in all areas of our lives. We'll become the victors and he'll become the victim. We'll be the ruler and he'll be subject under us. We'll trade our pity and pouting for explosive, intentional praise about what God has done, is doing, and what He's about to do. I'm on assignment, right here in Chapter One, to tell you that the struggle is almost over. The enemy knows he'll never win if _we_ don't give him the power, authority, and ultimate victory in our lives.

Now, I don't know when the change will come for you. However, I KNOW, by faith, things will get better. The children are going to get better. The marriage will survive (and if it's God will that the marriage doesn't survive, YOU will). The finances will become stable. Your health will get better. I believe the Lord will heal and restore you. The job situation will turn in your favor. However, you've got to hang in there until it happens.

Recently, I was traveling on US Highway 72 near my home when we ran into a traffic snarl. We only traveled about 50 yards in about 30 minutes. There was a driver behind me that obviously had road rage. He stuck his head out of the window cursing (like that would help). He zig-zagged behind me (like that would help). He blew his horn consistently (like that would help). He revved his engine (like that would help). He banged on his steering wheel like a crazed man (like that would help). He continued this for

Decisions

more than a half hour. Finally, about 10 yards ahead I saw where a lane had been closed for construction. Just beyond there I saw open road ready for two lane traffic. Finally, the traffic jam was about to be over. Suddenly Mr. Road Rage (please tell me this wasn't you) jetted through the median, spun around kicking up dirt and gravel (this man kicked rocks on my clean truck…smh), and sped back the other way. I wanted to scream, *"Dude, you waited this long only to turn around. You could see things were about to get better. You turned around just before we broke out of this jam!"* Now, that's my word to YOU! Don't you dare quit this walk of faith! Don't even think about going negative on me! Resist the urge to throw yourself a pity party! Don't do something irrational and illogical just to make things "better" for the moment. Don't even think about not going to Church. Get it out of your mind to stay at home and "get yourself together." I'll tell you like I wanted to tell Mr. Road Rage: *"Dude (or dudette), you've waited this long. You've come too far. You're oh so close to breaking out of your situation. Please don't turn around now. The atmosphere is shifting….so don't you!"*

Notes *and* Personal Reflections: My Head vs. My Heart

TWO

PRODUCTIVE UNDER PRESSURE

"But the more the Egyptians oppressed them, the more quickly the Israelites multiplied! The Egyptians quickly became alarmed..." **Exodus 1:12 NLT**

Pharaoh had to do something immediately. The insecurity about Israel's potential invoked the king to a level of unrivaled cruelty. Pharaoh placed relentless slave drivers over Israel *"hoping to wear them down under heavy burdens." (Exodus 1:11).* The slaves were forced to build major supply houses for the king. I can imagine Pharaoh emailing one of the slave drivers. It probably read, *"Break Israel down. Work them 'til they drop. Make it bad for them. Then that will stop them from making so many babies."* The king was sure that intense labor would limit Israel from doing anything else—including reproducing. However, he underestimated God's people. The text says, *"But the more the Egyptians oppressed them, the more quickly the Israelites multiplied."* Okay, you didn't get that! Let's try it this way: the more evil to come Israel's way, the more they were elevated. The more Pharaoh tried to break them down, the more Israel was breaking out. The more this man tried to limit Israel, the more the Lord lifted His people. Israel teaches us to *go forth* even when we are *going through*.

Decisions

That's a word for you today, my friend. Pharaoh thought oppressing, mistreating, abusing, & taking Israel through unbearable changes would shut them down. Instead, the struggle stirred them up. Likewise, Satan thinks that the oppression and depression that he's authored over your life is going to shut you down. He's tickled because he thinks the mistreatment and misunderstandings he has directed your way are going to mess you up. He's convinced the changes in your finances, your health, and certain situations in your life are going to turn you way from God. He just knows that the pressure he's applying is going to drive you away from God's purpose for your life. However, what he doesn't know is this: the God in you makes you determined to *go forth* even while you're *going through!* Israel got GREATER while going through. Go ahead and slap yourself high five and speak words of affirmation over your own life, *"I'll get greater while going through."* Yes, life's burdens may come. Yes, health issues may bring about some major changes in your life. Sure, the layoff will hurt. Without a doubt, if your finances are strained you'll feel it. Of course being betrayed and mistreated hurts your heart. I know that certain circumstances throw us all for a loop. The death of a dear loved one will sting for quite awhile. Still, keep your head high. Keep the smile on your face and know that if you *go forth* while going through, you'll be GREATER in the end. Like Israel when it came to their populating the land, I see your confidence multiplied. I see your faith multiplied. I see your determination multiplied. I see your self esteem multiplied. I see your appreciation for all God has done and continues to do for you, even when it comes to

Decisions

small things—multiplied. You and I serve a GREAT God that specializes in using what He allows His people to go through to make them greater.

You may wonder, *"Antoyne, how can you be so sure that God will always prevail when the enemy comes against His people."* Well, the simple answer is that I've seen Him do it in my life so many times before. However, the context of this text gives us a clearer theological picture. Please remember that God had already promised Abraham that He'd send the *"promised seed"*—the birth of a great nation. Also understand that no man, no enemy, no amount of evil, no hatred, no well- devised plan against God's people will forfeit God's plan. That's because to fight God's folks is to fight the Father Himself. At this point, Pharaoh hadn't figured out that he had picked a fight with God. It was a fight he couldn't win. If we are aligned with God and walking in His will, what He purposes for our lives will never be forfeited by any enemy. If God says the job is yours, it doesn't matter what negative venom someone else spews out about you. If God intends for your needs to be met, it doesn't matter how many stumbling blocks are thrown in your way. If our Father purposes you to be successful at a particular venture or in a particular field, it doesn't matter what the odds are and what the naysayers predict. What God has for you, it is for YOU!

So, what are we to do when unfortunate things happen in life? How are we to handle it when we're about to lose it because of how we're treated? Consider the issues as speed bumps and _not_ as roadblocks. When driving, a roadblock infers we can't go any farther. However, a speed bump—though it slows us down, shakes us a little, and creates a little noise—allows us to keep going forward. That said, the break up must be thought of us a speed bump on your way to a meaningful relationship. The financial strain is just a speed bump on the way to financial stability. The health issue is merely a speed bump on the way to a healthier lifestyle. The family and friends acting funny is merely a speed bump on your way to knowing God more intimately than ever before. Recognize life's speed bumps and keep going forward. You'll get where you're going and be a greater you when you get there if you keep the right attitude and stay determined to be productive even under pressure.

Consider one more thing from this particular passage. As we've noted before, Israel is still producing babies at a high rate even though Pharaoh's "hate rate" was at an all-time high as well. The revelation I'm directed to share with you is this: Israel never lost close intimacy with those they cared about regardless of what was happening. In the same manner, never allow the enemy to cancel friendships, displace trust, and to sift you away from those people God strategically placed in your life to bless you and encourage you. Satan loves it when you withdraw from everyone while you're dealing with tough times. DON'T DO THAT! Now, some folks MUST leave your life. In those times, you'll see God orchestrate their exit. However, at times we shy away from those God purposely plants to bless us. I'm not saying go blab everything about yourself and your situation to everyone. I'm not saying trust everybody with everything. However, know who God has allowed you to be intimately connected with. Maybe it's your mom, your dad, your sister, an aunt or uncle, a special cousin, or your very best friend. It could be (and should be) your wife or your husband. Maybe it's that special co-worker. The true essence of a meaningful, God-sent relationship is most often seen in times of struggle. God has people in place to love on you when you're at your lowest. He has some folks ready to hug you when you feel so alone and cold. He has some listening ears already primed and tuned to allow you to vent. He has a specially anointed mouth ready to release some words of wisdom to you. God touches people to give to you just what you need when you need it most. Sometimes, the person may do absolutely nothing but rub your back and say, *"It's okay."* However, that simple gesture could be God's key to keep you positive, productive, and at peace even in times of extreme pressure.

Antoyne L. Green

Most all, never lose sight of fact that regardless of what we face, when we face it, where we face it, and how long we have to face it we're never alone. Even when other people are nowhere to be found or are seemingly distant in even you presence, our God is just as close to us as we want Him and need Him to be. His power, protection, and provision are only a sincere heart, an earnest prayer, and a faith-filled praise away.

Notes *and* Personal Reflections: My Head vs. My Heart

THREE

COMMIT TO TRAIN YOUNG CHAMPIONS

"Then Pharaoh, the king of Egypt, gave this order to the Hebrew midwives, Shiprah and Puah: When you help the Hebrew women give birth, kill all the boys as soon as they are born. Allow only the baby girls to live. **Exodus 1:15-16 NLT**

Pharaoh had a plan to stop Israel from multiplying so quickly: kill every baby boy. This move made sense because if every male was eliminated, then basic biology tells us that human reproduction will eventually come to a halt. The king was determined to wipe out the younger generation of males. Unfortunately it's the same game plan that Satan is using today. The devil has an all out attack on our young men (yes, I'm keenly aware he's plotting against our young women too). The enemy's idea could be very simple. Many of us adults have matured and are continually maturing in God so that our faith and focus is growing day-by-day. Now, this doesn't mean our faith doesn't get weak. It does at times. This doesn't mean we don't have some sin issues at times. We do. This doesn't mean that we aren't susceptible to Satan's attacks. We certainly are. However, most mature Christians have a fixed heart and a made up mind to serve God and to remain in the security of His love, grace, mercy, peace, protection, and provision. However, Satan knows that many of our children are not as mature and strong and focused.

Decisions

Therefore, if he can negatively affect their generation he can negatively affect the future of the Body of Christ. Dr. R.A. Vernon from the Word Church in Cleveland, Ohio said it best when he declared, "Where there are no babies and young people there is no future." This is a very true statement.

It's a sad fact that so many of our young people are in the fight of their lives physically, mentally, emotionally, and spiritually. Babies are having babies setting up what could be a lifetime of struggle and dependence. The days of a good ole backyard fight with fists between a couple of friends who would quickly patch things up afterward are over. Now few kids fight. They war! Fists are for punks. Guns and knives are for "real men." Televisions, computers, other electronics, and even video games (whatever happened to Pac Man on an Atari 2600?) are training our kids. As a whole, kids today tend to not be very active and aren't very creative because they have every toy and gadget that does little to challenge them. Heck, a fun summer's day for me was riding bikes, playing basketball, shooting a BB gun, making mud pies, and etc. Now kids rarely go outside. All of this writes a sad and dangerous prescription for our kids that could jeopardize their futures in all facets and the future of the Body of Christ.

So what are we to do? We must "build" our boys and "build" our girls through encouragement, empowerment, and by being living examples in front of them. Our kids must know the societal, economic, and spiritual challenges they're bound to face. We must identify Satan as a real, formidable enemy of theirs. We must also let it be known that through the death, burial, and resurrection of Jesus Christ

Decisions

the enemy is ALREADY defeated. We must plant seeds of accountability, commitment, discipline, and faith in each child so that they have the needed tools to not only make it, but to succeed in whatever they endeavor. It's all about preparing our youth and young adults for what lies ahead.

I'm reminded of I Samuel 17:33 when Saul sent for David after learning that David had it in his mind to challenge the Philistine giant Goliath in a fight. Saul said to David, *"Don't be ridiculous! There is no way you can go against this Philistine. You are only a boy, and he has been in the army since he was a boy!"* Did you catch it? David said and knew, *"I can."* Saul said, *"You can't."* It's amazing that Saul saw the champion in Goliath, but didn't see the champion in David. Every, single child we come in contact with must know that he or she is a champion! Don't label them as troubled. Don't label them underprivileged. Don't' label them as a gang-banger. Don't label them as somebody's "mistake." Don't label them as a no-good, lost generation. No matter who the child is and what side of the tracks they come from, they must be told they are champions. Look back at the text for a moment. Saul tells David he can't beat Goliath because he was just a boy AND because Goliath had been a warrior since he was just a boy. Well, if Saul could be trained to be a champion as a child why couldn't David? We must train our young men and young women to be champions in every area of our lives. Their success later in life depends on it. *"Champion training"* says walk in confidence without being conceited. It says always say what you mean and mean what you say. Kids need to know that champions don't have much more than their integrity, honesty, and their word.

Decisions

Let's tell our kids that champions count the cost before saying *"Count me in."* Let's instill in our children that learning how to win sometimes is not nearly as important as learning how to lose. Let's instill in our young men that champions are courteous and respectful to women. Let our young women know that champions dress and talk decently and respectfully. Our kids must be taught that life is just like a bank: you'll only get out of it what you put into it. Most importantly, *"Champion Training"* instills into our young people that success is not in alcohol, drugs, promiscuous sexual activity, and running with the wrong crowd. We must let them know that there will be no lasting success independent of our real, true relationship with the Savior.

I know that this chapter may seem a bit "off message" from the entire book. However, I believe it's very much relevant. The king—

Israel's enemy—wanted to negatively affect the children. Heck, the king wanted to take all the boys out! Likewise, Satan wants to do the same to our kids today. That's why I challenge you to look at your precious kids, grandchildren, nephews, nieces, kids at church, and etc. and make this promise to them: **YOU SHALL LIVE LIFE ABUNDANTLY IN CHRIST!** Yes, our kids will make mistakes. Yes, they'll be like other kids and hit their *"rebellious, hard-headed, and 'you can't tell me anything' streak."* However, if they've been trained as champions in God, eventually they'll be victorious and successful in life and then train their children and grandchildren. It's time we break the enemy's cycle and abort his plans against our children. Our kids must know there is only one way to a truly blessed life. That's through Christ Jesus our Lord!

Notes *and* Personal Reflections: My Head vs. My Heart

FOUR

THE FEAR OF GOD PRODUCES THE FAVOR OF GOD

"But because the midwives feared God, they refused to obey the king and allow the boys to live, too." **Exodus 1:17 NLT**

The orders from Pharaoh were crystal clear. They heard them. They had a bloody, gruesome job to do. They were to become murderers of innocent Israelite baby boys. It appears that the midwives had no option but to obey the king's cruel orders. Then again, they did have another option—it was apparently the **ONLY** option for the midwives—**OBEY GOD!** Now some people have problems with the fact that midwives had the nerve and audacity to disobey a king. Now, the Bible is clear that we should obey those with authority and in authority. I'm not suggesting or advocating being some loose screw rebel who simply wants to do his or her own thing. However, there will be times in life when your faith and loyalty to God will be challenged by people. Believe me, my friend—you'll never lose by trusting and obeying our God. In this text, the midwives received orders from **A** king. However, the directions from **THE** King were totally opposite. So what is one to do when God's commands and man's commands are in conflict? Who should we follow? Always follow the directions of God. However, PLEASE

Decisions

keep this one fact in mind: if God said and ordered it, whatever "it" is will be decent, it will be in order, it will not be divisive (long-term anyway), it will not be destructive, and most of all it will not fail.

I'm reminded of one of the biggest faith walks I've ever taken. In January of 2000, God clearly instructed me to plant a new ministry in my hometown of Athens, AL. In June of that year the New Life Missionary Baptist Church was birthed. The Church's temporary building at its beginning and the location where we now worship is about two miles or so from my home Church. You can only imagine the barrage of negativity born out of public opinion. It was everything from I left my home Church and started a new Church because I was mad at the Pastor to I was a traitor and simply wanted to split the membership of my home Church.

Honestly, the talk was painful. After all, I did and still do love my home Church with all my heart. I was born into that Church. I gave my life to Christ there. I sang in the choir. Then I directed the Chancellor Choir for 12 years. I was an usher. I initiated the Media Ministry. My loyalty was there. Still, while there was *some* encouragement and positive feedback about beginning a new Ministry, the negativity was crazy! My pastor allowed me to preach one final message at my home Church and announce my intentions that same day. It appeared that the naysayers missed four very important words from my mouth—*"God directed me to…."* Either I was going to bow to the backlash or I was going to bow to my God and say, *"Yes, Lord."* Either I was going to be focused on hoping and trying to make people believe in me or I was going to be encouraged by the fact that God believed in me

Decisions

so much that He charged me with this major task. Either I was going to stay and wither because I would've been out of the will of God or I would move forward, be fruitful, and most of all live in joy and peace. Oh! Did I forget to tell you that I had no members? I had no money. I had no place to worship. I had no equipment—not even the first speaker, microphone, or even an offering plate. So either I was going to trust my logical thinking and the fears it produced or I was going to trust God. I chose to trust and obey God! Now, at the time of this writing, almost fourteen years later New Life Church is still doing God's work. She has some beautiful and anointed people in her. Our Ministry is a loving place filled with people who love God, His Church, and His people. No, we're not the biggest Church. No, we're not the most elaborate Church. However, WE ARE GOD'S

Church! Therefore, our obedience TO Him comes with an obligation FROM Him to take care of us, provide for us, and progress us forward as He sees fit.

I said all of that to encourage you to put your trust in God well above your trust in men. Think more about **God** believing in you than worrying about others believing in you. If God directs you, it's His obligation to supply your needs, sustain you, and strengthen you in all things. However, the midwives in the text teach us that it all begins with a fear of God. This doesn't suggest being scared of God; just submissive. Fear doesn't suggest we should retreat from God; just reverence Him as the Sovereign, true and living God. The fear of God keeps our focus on what delights Him and not on what delights others—even ourselves. It was the midwives' fear of God that caused them to let

Decisions

the baby boys live despite what Pharaoh ordered. It was their fear that caused them to stand boldly before the king as he interrogated them after he learned what the midwives had been doing *(verses 18-19)*. The reverent fear of God will always lead us to obey our Master and stand boldly before men. In return, God will honor our reverent fear of Him with favor upon our lives.

The Bible says in verse 20 that God blessed the midwives. Verse 21 is more descript in that it says, *"And because the midwives feared God, he gave them families of their own."* Look at this. The midwives' fear of God directed them to allow the Israelite baby boys to live. In return God showed the midwives favor by blessing them with families of their own. Every baby boy they let live was a seed sown into their own divine destiny. They sowed life and God blessed them with lives—families—that would be dear to them. Likewise our reverent fear of God will produce favor upon our lives because we'll always sow faith seeds into our destiny. Our reverent fear of God will cause us to believe Him, celebrate Him, do as He directs us, have faith in Him, and so much more. In return, we'll reap a harvest of blessings upon our lives. God keeps those who fear Him. God blesses those who fear Him. God opens doors for those whose hearts are open to His direction. God sustains those who reckon that there is no substitution for God and His commands. God provides for those who are proven loyal to Him. God trusts those with favor and blessings who have proven that they truly trust Him.

However, the most important aspect of the midwives' obedience is found in verse 20, *"….and the Israelites continued to multiply,*

Decisions

growing more and more powerful." When the midwives obeyed God, it opened the door for God's purpose and plan to continue. He wanted Israel to multiply. He wanted Israel to grow more powerful. This couldn't have happened if all the males were killed at birth. The midwives teach us a very important lesson here. Everything we do in life should further God's plan and purpose. If God is not glorified, it's not worth it. If God's kingdom is not advanced, it's not worth it. If God's people are not blessed, it's not worth it. In all we do and all we say, we should ask ourselves one important question, *"Do my thoughts, words, attitude, and actions match up with what God is doing and wants to do in my life and in my surroundings?"* Our prayers daily should be filled with the words of Bishop Paul S. Morton's song, *"Lord, whatever you're doing in this season please don't do it without me!"* However, remember that if God grants us the privilege of being included in His plans, He doesn't always provide details of what's to come. He just needs willing workers who believe that everything God leads us to, He'll lead us through. He desires faith-filled believers that understand that truly every, single thing we do for God has purpose for His glory. He also desires those people filled with reverent fear who aren't scared to be scrutinized for being sincere in the work of God. In other words, friend God is looking for you. God believes in you. Walk in your reverent fear of Him and watch His favor fall upon you.

Notes *and* Personal Reflections: My Head vs. My Heart

FIVE

THE BEAUTIFUL BLESSING

"During this time, a man and a woman from the tribe of Levi got married. The woman became pregnant and gave birth to a son. She saw what a beautiful baby he was..." **Exodus 2:1-2 NLT**

Maybe it was an answer to a prayer. Maybe it was completely unexpected. Maybe it was a longtime coming. Maybe you had no clue it was coming. I think it's safe to assume that most all of us have received or achieved a great blessing that meant so much to us. You possibly know how it feels to get that dream vehicle. You keep it washed on the outside and without lint or dust on the inside. Or maybe you remember finally closing on your dream home. You couldn't vacuum the carpet enough. Every cushion had to be in place. By no means could there be a wrinkle in the perfectly made bed. Then maybe it was the ten little fingers and toes of your precious child or grandchild that melted your heart. There would be nothing too good for him or there would be nothing you wouldn't do for her. The idea here is that life presents many, many blessings that touch our heart. For most people, it's just natural to develop an affection and intimacy with things and people that touch and move our lives.

This was the case with Amram and Jochebed. They gave birth to a little boy we know as Moses. As most little children do, Moses instantly arrested the heart of his parents, especially his mother. The text says that Jochebed *"saw what a beautiful baby he was."* While we certainly take the text at its word, we know how mothers are with their children! If no one else thought Moses was beautiful, Jochebed did. If no one else thought Moses was precious, Jochebed did. If no one else instantly fell in love with Moses, we can rest assured that Jochebed did. This baby was a blessing that came to her from God. This is a blessing that God birthed out of her. So naturally, Jochebed would see things a bit differently than anyone else. The revelation here is simple. When it comes to the blessings of God, we must have "Jochebed Vision." If the Lord gives it to us, it's precious. If the Lord makes a way for the blessing to happen, it's precious. If the Lord gives us the vision for great things and the strength to attain and accomplish great things, those things are precious. If the Lord does it for us, performs a miracle on our behalf, and provides us with it, it must be precious. Again, the blessing may be result of a prayer answered. Then again, the blessing may be unexpected grace and favor shown to you. Regardless, we must reckon God's blessings as truly precious to us. Did Jochebed have the only beautiful baby ever? Of course not. However, to her there couldn't be any other baby more precious and beautiful than hers.

Friend, true appreciation for the blessings of God upon our lives creates an affection and an attitude that believes God has graced us with the very best. People with this mentality and attitude don't complain about much. We celebrate the things, the people the Lord has blessed us to have in our lives, the positions, and blessed situations that the Lord has placed us in. Let me go ahead and clear the air right now

Decisions

about a few things: there is not a more beautiful woman alive than Felicia Green. My wife is God-sent just for me. There are not any better children than Jasmynn, Kaleb, and Emani. There is no better mother created than Deloris Green. George Green should win "Father of the Year" every year. Andrea Willis should take home the best "Big Sis" award. Rosie French is heaven's "premium" granny! There are no other in-laws greater than Reverend Fred and Eleanor Batts. Our home is on point. I'm loving my Toyota Sequoia (it's my 'man' truck). New Life Church is the greatest Church this side of Heaven. The anointing on my life is the most precious possession I own. Now, to someone who just casually reads this, it appears that I'm arrogant, conceited, braggadocio, and really stuck on me and mine! To the contrary! It's that I agree with the song we often sing at the New Life Church.

Its lyrics say, *"I'm blessed. God knows I'm blessed. When I look all around me, I realize I'm blessed. Over and over, the Lord keeps on blessing me. I can't explain it. It's so amazing. The Lord keeps on blessing me!"* My appreciation for the Lord's blessing keeps me saying within myself, *"There can't be anything greater than this because GOD made it happen."* The people listed above are not perfect. They're flawed like we all are; but they're God's blessing to me. The things listed above are not all that; but they're mine because God gave them to me. Friend, the "Jochebed Vision" lets you look all around, clearly see the blessings of God upon your life, and then declare them as beautiful and precious. Just take a moment and think of all the people, things, and achievements that God has allowed to affect and shape your life in a great way. Aren't they precious? Well, thank God for all

Decisions

He's done. Not long ago, my son and I were driving and the lane I was in was closing. I put on my signal to get over and after a few cars passed, a nice lady let me over in front of her. I looked back in the mirror, and then waved my hand. Kaleb inquired as to what I was doing. I told him that the nice lady had just allowed me to get over in front of her and that the right thing to do was to look back at the one who blessed me and wave my hand to tell them *"Thank You."* I just felt that one. Friend, have you started waving to God yet? You're breathing. It's a beautiful thing. Tell Him thank you. You've got a reasonable portion of health and strength. It's a beautiful thing. You get it, my friend. If you can **THINK** of God's blessings to you, then you certainly ought to **THANK** God for all He's done, all He's doing, and all He's going to do. In your mind, there should be no greater spouse than yours. There aren't any greater and cuter kids than yours. The job you have is blessing. Your church is the bomb! Your home is just that—a home! Your car is uniquely fitted for you! There's nobody like your family! It's not arrogance. It's appreciation. Friend, behold the blessings upon your life and call them beautiful.

Notes *and* Personal Reflections: My Head vs. My Heart

SIX

THE STRUGGLE WITHIN

"But when she could no longer hide him, she got a little basket made of papyrus reeds and waterproofed it with tar and pitch. She put the baby in the basket and laid it among the reeds along the edge of the Nile River." **Exodus 2:3 NLT**

In the introduction to this book, I stated that one of the greatest conflicts in life is when there is a disagreement and subsequent battle between our heads and hearts. Often times what _needs_ to be done and what _we want_ to do are two different things. Often our _desires_ produce a completely different roadmap than the Lord's *direction.* Inner conflicts like this serve as the genesis for many emotionally charged and frustrating days. They create some tearful, sleepless, & restless nights.

I think it's safe to assume that Jochebed felt some of the pains and experienced some of the same scenarios described above. In the text Moses had just turned three months old. He's a cute little baby—that's got a target on his back. He's a precious little child—with a death warrant signed against him. He's an innocent little child—with an insecure king for an enemy. After his encounter with the midwives, Pharaoh ordered that every male Israelite child be thrown into the Nile River (Exodus 1:22). Obviously Moses fitted that description. However, for three months Jochebed had nurtured Moses and managed to keep him hidden. Still, just like any other child,

Decisions

Moses was a growing boy. His cries got louder. The chances of the wrong people hearing him were greater now. The chances of the wrong people spotting him some kind of way were greater after three months. Moses was in danger and Jochebed knew it. So what was this mother to do? It's safe to assume that she loved this baby with her whole heart. We know that mothers tend to have an unmatched and indescribable love toward their kids. They bond, sight unseen, for nine months. That's where the motherly seed of love is planted. Then the love grows greater when mom sets her eyes on that precious child after birth. No doubt Jochebed loved little Moses; but what was she to do with him once it become hard, if not impossible, to keep Moses hidden? I'm sure one train of thought was, *"I'll keep him and try to do a better job keeping him hidden."* Then another mind said, *"As much as it will affect me emotionally, it's better for Moses if I get him out of here and find a way to preserve my baby's life."* Oh what a struggle this had to have been. I imagine Jochebed thought one thing; but her heart believed another. That which seemed logical may not have necessarily been the right thing to do. That which was desired was likely in conflict with the direction she should take.

On some level or another, we all know what it means to have a deep, serious struggle within. We arrive at a crossroad of decision with, quite frankly, no clear path of what we're going to do. I'm sure this book will come into the hands of some people who have had to make some serious, life changing decisions in which there may have been disagreements with others and disagreements deep with himself or herself. Fact is, someone who will read this book has had

Decisions

to make or is possibly pondering a deep decision of whether to abort a child, birth the child and do their best to raise it, or birth the baby and offer it for adoption. Someone has lost or is losing sleeping trying to figure out if willpower is enough to break the addiction or if rehabilitation and professional help is the way to go. Someone wants to marry the love of their heart; but is fearful based on signs and information that have come forth. Someone wants to leave the abuse. However, fear of the abuser keeps arresting her (or his) mind and heart. Maybe you think it's time for change in your life. However, part of you says it's best to stay at exactly where you are. Maybe you think it's time to move to the next job. Still there is part of you that says losing seniority, vacation time, and the easy schedule you enjoy is too much give up. Do you have the surgery or not? Do you buy the car or home now or not? Do you speak to a loved one or friend about something that they need to know, knowing it may not be well received or not? Do you cash out your retirement and 401K or not? Do you vote for this candidate, his or her rival, or neither of them? Friend, this list could go on infinitely. The idea here is very simple: we all must learn how to confront and deal with inner struggles.

One thing is for sure—we can't act like the struggles don't exist or will go away on their own. Jochebed teaches us that. She knew that Moses had reached an age where his life was going to be in serious jeopardy. She knew that she may not be able to save him. This was a real crisis that required real attention. Likewise, life often forces us to admit, whether we want to or not, when we are at a crossroads and when there is a struggle in our minds and hearts. We

Decisions

must face the tough decisions because they are not going away. I was watching the news one day and a story spotlighted this elderly man who fulfilled his life dream of skydiving. Jumping out of an airplane was on the man's "bucket list." Well, he finally got up the nerve, paid his money, boarded the plane, and off into the blue skies he went. Cameras were attached to the plane and to the elderly gentleman to record the special moment. Once high in the sky, the man jumped out of the plane. The cameras showed the man flailing his arms and continually saying, "This is so beautiful." The man made a picture-perfect landing. Once on the ground he was interviewed and asked was he afraid. He stood tall, pointed to a man right beside him and said, *"No. As long as I was connected to him I knew somebody was right there with me during the fall."* Of course, he was referring to his skydiving instructor. This man's words blessed me and I hope they bless you. Be sure you're connected to the Sovereign God. Be sure you never attempt to make a decision or take any action without being firmly secured IN Him and TO Him. That way, though the decisions may be tough and the battle within may be long, tiring, and frustrating you're not going through it alone! God's got you. If you listen, God will speak to your heart and spirit. If you wait patiently, God will set some things in motion to confirm to you that it's Him working on your behalf. If you don't let desperation drive you, God will comfort you and direct you into HIS path for your life. In your weakness, God will show you just how strong He is. When the issue seems bigger than life, God will show you just how big He is. When the struggle within reaches a level of intensity that you've never experienced before, remember you're connected to Jehovah

Decisions

Shalom! He's the Almighty God who is your peace! When you feel so alone, remember you're connected to Jehovah Shammah! He's the true and living God who is everywhere at the same time. If you enjoy a true "love relationship" with God, you never have to search for Him or wonder if He's there. The Psalmist makes that clear when he penned Psalm 46:1, *"God is our refuge and strength, **always ready** to help in times of trouble."* Friend, when we reach the crossroads of life two things are sure: the peace of God will keep us while the Spirit of God directs us.

Notes *and* Personal Reflections: My Head vs. My Heart

SEVEN

HE [SHE] WON'T DROWN

"...but when she could no longer hide him, she got a little basket made of papyrus reeds and waterproofed it with tar and pitch." **Exodus 2:3a NLT**

So the decision is made. Jochebed is going to save Moses' life by "letting him go." Can't you just see the pain in this mother's face? Can't you see the tears gently rolling down her cheeks? Can't you hear the little whimper as she continues to make the little basket for Moses that will also serve as his personal boat in the

Nile? But wait! Did you notice *how* Jochebed constructed the basket? She tightly wove papyrus reeds and then pasted slimy, sticky tar and pitch all over it. Jochebed made a waterproof boat for her son. Catch the revelation here. Though she was about to put Moses in the basket and put the basket in the river, Jochebed assured that the basket was not going to sink. Jochebed assured that, though little Moses was likely about to face a difficult situation in the Nile, he was going to be safe. I believe this loving mother's mindset basically said, *"I'm not going to let my child drown!"*

Man, if only we had a way to know exactly what was on Jochebed's mind at this point! I wish we had just a notion of what her heart really felt. Still, there is so much to glean here. First, consider that fact that up to this point this mother had done all she could for Moses. She

Decisions

birthed him. She nursed him. She lovingly nurtured him. She kept him safely hidden. She provided for him. Jochebed did all she could possibly do for her son. However, the time had come for her to _release_ him. Though painful, it was Moses' best chance of survival. Though so difficult, she couldn't hold him anymore. Jochebed's love for Moses was still very true and very strong. Still it was time to trust her decision and trust the preparations she had meticulously and tirelessly made for her son. It was time to release him. It was time to trust God in the matter.

I think this is an area many of us have found ourselves in before. Some of us are still in this difficult place. We can, as my late great Aunt Martha used to say, love people "so hard" that it becomes difficult—if not almost impossible—to step back and "let them go." Maybe the parents who have a child that continually gets into trouble fit this profile. Maybe the parents who've given their child everything and have gotten nothing but disrespect back fit this profile. Maybe the single mom who has sacrificed so much so her child could have everything he needed and much of what he wanted, yet he is so unappreciative fits this profile. Maybe the dad who worked tirelessly to provide for the apple of his eye—his baby girl—only to be met with rebellion from her fits this profile. Conversely, maybe the parents who have raised their kids as best as they could all their lives and now the "little birds" are about to "fly away" to college fit this description. Or maybe it's the dad who walks his daughter down the aisle and places his "Punkin's" hand in the hand of another man fits this description. Still, it could be the mom who has admittedly spoiled her

Decisions

baby boy and who lights the first candle at her son's wedding fits this description. While each of these scenarios is a bit different, the prevailing principle is the same. In each instance, just like Jochebed, you have parents who reach the point that it's time to let their children go. I had no intention of shifting into this area, but the Spirit would have me to write this to bless and encourage someone who has already had to let go or is facing that challenge now. In the fall of 2013, Jasmynn, our oldest child, enrolled in college. For weeks, maybe even months, prior to Jazz going away, I saw she and my wife buying things for college. For days I saw Jazz slowly but surely packing her things getting ready for the big move. Then that fateful day in August came. It was move-in day for the freshmen. Felicia and Jazz went on down to Birmingham early that morning. I stayed in Huntsville because our son

Antoyne L. Green

Kaleb had a football game. Kaleb, Emani, and I were to go to Birmingham the minute the game was over. Truth is, I just remember that Kaleb's team lost. I don't remember much more about that game. Why? It's because my mind was so preoccupied with the fact that this precious little girl who was only six when I married her mom was leaving home. This was the little thumb-sucking girl who would come and sit in my lap without notice. This was the child who would fall asleep in my arms while she was rubbing my earlobes or my elbow. This was the child-turned-young lady who did things kids and teenagers tend to do; but was never an ounce of trouble. This was the young lady we all were (and still are) so proud of. She was about to leave home! After Kaleb's game we made the trek to Birmingham. Jazz and Felicia had already gotten her settled into the room. We talked for a while

Decisions

and then it was time to go. It was time to leave Jazz in Birmingham. I looked and Jazz was red in the face with a little smile of uncertainty. I looked at Felicia—tears. I looked at Kaleb—tears. I looked at Emani—tears. I know what you're thinking—NO, I didn't cry; but my heart was breaking. Once we got home, it was time to meditate on preaching in our Sunday worship the next morning. I prayed and asked God to settle my mind, heart, and spirit regarding Jazz moving out. Then it came to me. From the moment Jazz cried out in the world on February 15, 1995, Felicia, my wife's parents, and others had nurtured her and loved her. Then from the time we got married in 2001 until now my parents, other family members, and I have had the privilege of joining in the nurturing process. Jazz had been trained for life. She had been raised in Christ. She was taught integrity, character, self-respect, and discipline. She was taught right and wrong. She was taught how to be a lady. She had been "trained up in the way that she should go" (Proverbs 22:6). In other words, we had done like Jochebed. We had prepared Jazz for her new journey. We were releasing her. However, we assured that our baby *"would not drown"* in life. Has she and is she going to bump her head a few times? Sure. Maybe make a bad decision or two? Definitely. Has she and will she learn a few things the hard way? It's almost certain. However, we had to trust we had prepared her. It was time to let her go. It was time to trust God to care for her, keep her, and mature her.

I said all of that as encouragement to those who have had or possibly is having a hard time letting go of a child or loved one. If you've raised them the best you can, loved on them

Decisions

unconditionally, have always been there for them, have been a positive example before them, taught them right from wrong, instilled in them Godly character and integrity, shown them a positive work ethic and so much more about life, then you have prepared them for what's to come. They're not going to drown! It's hard to let go. However, there comes a time and a season where you're simply going to have to trust that what you've instilled in them will be their compass in life. You're going to have to trust that God will care for and keep them. You're going to have to trust that God will continue to mature them first of all in the things of the Kingdom and then in life. We must have confidence in the positive things we've instilled in others and confidence in God to move in their lives. Then we can be at peace. No matter what happens, how many mistakes are made, and how many different issues life presents them, we can sit back and confidently believe and say, *"God's got my child....my brother....my sister....my cousin.....my best friend & etc. They've been prepared and they will not drown!"*

Notes *and* Personal Reflections: My Head vs. My Heart

EIGHT

KEPT

"...she put the baby in the basket and laid it among the reeds along the edge of the Nile River." **Exodus 2:3b NLT**

Hard decisions are hard decisions. Emotional decisions normally tap into just about every emotional fiber that there is. If we're not careful we'll allow difficulty to drive us to desperation. In turn, our response in times of hurt and crisis will often be without careful, thoughtful, and prayerful planning and preparation. However, this is not the case with

Jochebed. That's evident in the last chapter just from how she made the basket that she'd eventually put Moses in. It's also evident in this portion of the text when Jochebed carefully places the basket into the river's edge. This loving mother made sure that in a time of literal uncertainty and instability that her baby boy was _covered_ and was _kept._ Friend—if you're searching for hope and optimism during the most difficult and unpredictable times, this chapter is just for you.

Jochebed settled Moses in his custom-made basket and then placed the basket in the reeds along the riverbanks of the Nile. The place where we find reasons to rejoice is "in the reeds." Understand that reeds tend to grow densely along waterfronts and riverbanks. A patch of reeds can be very thick. That means when Jochebed placed the basket containing

Decisions

Moses into the reeds, she put her son in position that not only would he not sink and drown, but he wouldn't be swept away very fast and harshly by the currents of the Nile. The reeds assured that baby Moses was _kept_ despite the waves and currents that were prevalent. If Moses were alive today, I believe he'd be shouting, *"I rejoice in the reeds! They kept me!"* Friend, in the same manner that Moses would have a bona fide reason to rejoice because his mother ensured he was kept, we have a reason to walk in a strong faith that our Father will keep us. Fast forward a moment to Moses' time as an adult. Do you remember when God charged him to go to Egypt and tell Pharaoh to let His people go? Moses asked God who he should say sent him. God had a two word response that was more than sufficient. God told Moses to tell them, "I AM" sent you! That simple response gives us reason to rejoice. "I AM," when it comes to describing the presence, power, and nature of God, gives us a true sense of the breadth and depth of His Sovereignty. "I AM" basically says, *"There is absolutely nothing that I am not. There is nowhere that I am not. There is nothing that I am not able to do. I AM all things. I AM everything."* In this example, God was Liberator. He was Rescuer. He was Commander In Chief. He was Ruler over ALL things! God was God. Guess what my friend—He's STILL all of those things and more! Yeah, right about here is a good place to rejoice! God will keep us when waves and currents of live try to sweep away from our faith, our family, and our focus. In sickness, God's a keeper! During the fallout of broken relationships, God's a keeper! During the government shutdown, sequestration and lay-offs, God's a keeper! In times of danger, God's a

Decisions

keeper. During the time of financial hardship, God's a keeper! When the enemy is waging every spiritual attack possible, God's a keeper! You think and feel like you're about to lose your mind, God's a keeper! Nobody seems to understand; meaning nobody can comfort or help you, God's a keeper! Yes, you get it now! The Great *"I AM"* is able to do every possible thing you need done. He's able to minister to you in whatever capacity you need Him to. God's a keeper. Somebody is still not convinced. Take a moment and reflect back over your life. How many times has God been your Provider? How many times has God been your Healer? How many times has God been your Comforter? How many times has God been your Peace? How many times has God been your Faithful Friend? How many times has God been your Rock? How many times has God fought your battles? Well, if you can remember *those* times, you can rejoice *at all times.* One of attributes of God is that He is immutable. That means He doesn't change at all (Hebrews 13:8). If He healed you before, He's still healing now! If He's made a way for you before, He's still making ways now. If He's put your enemies in check before, they're still no match for our God now! If He's given you peace during a most difficult time before, He's still Jehovah-Shalom—our Peace—now! If He's worked one miracle, He'll work another miracle in His own time and His own way. Bottom line is this: you're still here because God has *kept* you from being swept away! Now shout! Why?!! Because He's still our keeper! I know you're likely familiar with the story of the three Hebrew Boys—Shadrach, Meshach, and Abednego—being thrown into the fiery furnace. You know, as miraculous as it was for God to deliver them

Decisions

from the fiery furnace, I've come to the conclusion that we should've known He would from the very beginning. You see, back in biblical times the name a person was often considered as a testimony of their early years and a prophetic view of their latter years. That said, a simple study of the *Hebrew* names of the Hebrew boys gives us some great insight. Shadrach's Hebrew name was Hananiah which means *"Jehovah is gracious."* Meshach's Hebrew name was Mishael which means *"high places; who is what God is."* Abednego's Hebrew name was Azariah which means *"Jehovah is a keeper; hath helped."* No wonder God delivered the Hebrew boys. Their names said it all—*Jehovah is gracious, Who is what God is, and Jehovah is a keeper!"* The names of these three were direct testimonies of God character and nature. That said, I believe maybe Hananiah is reading this book right now—you KNOW God is gracious! Maybe it's Mishael reading this book—you KNOW you're striving to be just as God would have you to be. Then again, maybe it's Azariah reading this book—you KNOW that your God is a keeper! Yeah, I feel that too! That's why we should rejoice at all times. Even when we don't have a clue *how* God will work things out, we should know within our hearts that *He will* work things out. Even though we can't always stop the storms from coming in our lives, we can rejoice in the fact that God will keep us. I agree with the lyrics of the popular song by Douglas Miller, *"Though the storms keep on raging in my life and sometimes it hard to tell the night from day. Still the hope that lies within reassures as I keep my eyes upon the distant shore. I know He'll lead me safely to that blessed place He has prepared. If the storms don't cease and if the winds keep on*

Decisions

blowing in my life—my soul has been anchored in the Lord!"

Notes *and* Personal Reflections: My Head vs. My Heart

NINE

COVERED

"...she put the baby in the basket and laid it among the reeds along the edge of the Nile River." **Exodus 2:3b NLT**

When you really love someone you'll go to the ends of the earth to show that love. I think Jochebed has certainly done that for baby Moses. Review for a moment. She gave birth to him. She nurtured and kept him hidden from danger for three months. She put his best interest ahead of her emotions. She built a waterproof basket so Moses wouldn't sink and drown in the Nile. She placed the basket in thick reeds so the basket wouldn't be swept away in the waves and currents. There is no doubt that Jochebed's love for Moses is on display. Still it goes a bit further. When Jochebed placed the basket in the reeds, she ensured not only that her baby wouldn't be swept away, but also that Moses wouldn't be scorched by the sun or be easy prey for predators. Jochebed made sure her child was _covered._ You see, the reeds were typically thick and strong at the bottom. However, they grew tall and had large, wide leaves at the top. So when Jochebed put Moses' basket in the reeds, the leaves covered her child. That's my encouragement to you, my friend. Whomever or whatever it is that you love, **cover them!** Cover your children. Cover your spouse. Cover your siblings. Cover your parents. Cover other family members. Cover your significant

Decisions

other. Cover your Pastor. Cover the members of your Church. Don't leave those you love to fend for themselves in life. Cover them. You don't have to be near them to cover them. You don't have to know everything concerning them to cover them. In actuality, you don't even have to talk to them to cover them. If you have a relationship with God our Father through Jesus Christ, you can cover those people and those things dear to you! Our friend Job shows us this.

In the first chapter of Job, it says that Job's kids had birthday parties each year. The parties were apparently, as the kids say these days, *"turned up!"* Job's kids would eat and drink. After the parties were over, Job would purify his kids by offering a burnt offering for each of them. Job did this because he thought. *"Perhaps my children have sinned and have cursed God in their hearts." (Job 1:4-5).* The Bible never indicates that Job attended the parties. However, he did _cover_ his children through his meditation and burnt offerings. He didn't want to take a chance that his kids' relationship with God has been broken in any way. Well, maybe we don't offer burnt offerings on behalf of others these days. However, we can and should still cover those dear to us through prayer. Yes, I'm fully aware that people—particularly grown people—have minds of their own and have to make conscious choices on their own. I'm also very much aware that no matter what we do, there are some things that those we love must learn and endure on their own. However, that doesn't stop us from bathing them in our prayers. As a Pastor, I want to be a good teacher, preacher, and administrator. However, the people I pastor also need me to cover them as an awfully good prayer intercessor. As a Father, I do

Decisions

my best to provide for and support my family. I try to be a good, Godly example for my wife and children. However, they also need me to cover them as an intercessor. I pray for those I love. I pray for those dear to me. I pray for those I have relationship with. I also pray for those I don't know. We're called to cover others. While I've always known this, I witnessed it up close and personal the last couple of years. We had a precious member of our Church named NaTanya Dean. Natanya was one of the most faithful members New Life has ever had. A couple of years ago she was diagnosed with breast cancer. This young lady fought the cancer like a heavyweight champ—twice! After numerous treatments and many long days and nights the breast cancer was finally declared gone! However, unbeknownst to anyone, while the cancer had been eradicated from her breasts, it had spread to her liver. The diagnosis came in early November 2013. It was going to be a battle of battles; but we all figured Tanya would win this one too. Our Church prayed for our sister and friend consistently. Daily my wife and I prayed for Tanya. We had her covered! However, there was **_nobody_** who covered Tanya like her parents, Jerry and Jean Dean. I have said this both publicly and privately and I'll say it in this writing: "I have learned so many spiritual lessons from these two people!" Daily Mr. Dean and I would communicate (most often by text) regarding how Tanya's day had been. Each day, this loving father would tell me the highs and lows of the day. Then he would tell me *specifically* what our point of agreement in prayer was to be. One day it may have been for Tanya to have more strength. The next day the point of agreement may have been for Tanya's

Decisions

pain to subside and for good lab results. The prayer requests varied from day-to-day and sometimes throughout the same day. Yet, this father and mother kept their daughter covered in prayer. Shortly after the diagnosis of the liver cancer, I had the privilege of being at Tanya's bedside with her parents and their Pastor. We anointed her with oil and then bathed her—covered her—in an intense, faith-filled time of prayer. This praying and believing occurred just about every time I visited her. I also remember her parents even sent out a prayer request email in which it asked all who loved Tanya to stand in agreement on certain points of emphasis. It was very clear to me that this family believes God! It was clear that this family wasn't going to let Tanya fight these battles on her own! They stood with her and beside her! They covered their child in prayer endlessly.

As is turned out, it was not the perfect will of God that Tanya would be healed on earth. She transitioned to be the Lord on December 30, 2013. However, even in her last moments on earth, I stood at Tanya's bedside with Mr. Dean and his family as he led us in prayer and continued to cover her and then sweetly submit her to whatever God's will would ultimately be. While God's will was different than all of our desires, I learned so much from this family. Throughout her entire ordeal, Tanya covered _herself!_ She was strong, full of faith, and truly believed her healing would come *"on this side."* She never wavered in that belief. There was no pity party. There was no negativity. She accepted what God allowed as a powerful woman of faith and believed that God would see her through it. From Tanya's parents and siblings, I learned that there is no such thing as extreme when it comes

Decisions

to being there for those you love and covering them in prayer and support. Ultimately, a couple of hours before Tanya transitioned, Mr. Dean pulled a Jochebed. He still believed God for Tanya's healing. However, he also was also humbly submissive to however God chose to bring Tanya's healing. In essence, he placed his baby girl *"among the reeds"* and trusted that God had her covered.

Mr. Dean and all of us have a great example of One who covers those He loves. Our Lord has covered us all of our lives and continues to do so even now. He does it two ways: through prayer and also practically. In Luke 22:31-32, Jesus told Peter that Satan wanted him. Our Lord informed Peter that enemy wanted to *"sift you as wheat."* Then the Jesus says, *"But I have prayed for [you]....."* In other words, Jesus told Peter, *"You've got a real enemy that is really determined to take you down! But don't worry. I've got you covered! I have prayed you!"* Isn't it good news that we're on Heaven's prayer list when it also appears that we're on hell's hit list? Our Lord has us covered. He's prayed for us. Now He's seated on the right hand of God interceding for us. He's pleading our case before the God the Father. Even when we don't know what's best, Jesus does and makes our case. We're covered! Even when we don't have the words to say or knowledge of what we should pray for, the Holy Spirit does and intercedes on our behalf. We're covered! When the enemy, also known as the Accuser of the Brethren, tries to discredit us, our lives, our motives, and etc. before God, Jesus claims us as His own. We're covered. Friend, the Lord Jesus never leaves us uncovered! He never quits advocating on our behalf. The Spirit never quits His intercession on

Decisions

our behalf! Jesus tells God the Father, *"He's mine. She's mine. They've accepted me as Christ, Savior, and Lord!"* The Spirit says, *"Green could only manage to muster out a 'Lord have mercy!' But what He really meant was, "Lord, direct me as I deal with this difficult situation."* Hey, if I were you I'd go ahead and celebrate now. We're covered through prayer and intercession.

We're also covered practically. Remember I told you that the reeds have the large, fan-like leaves that would provide shade from the sun and covering from predators. Well, our Lord is our "leaf." Friend, you and I are still breathing because the Lord's been our shelter! Yes, I know that many unpleasant and unforeseen things may have transpired in your life. However, rest assured that there have been and will be many more things aimed directly at you that you'll never see, feel, or be affected by. That's because

God's covering you! It's because of your covering that many people who meant you no good left you alone or never approached you at all. It's because of your covering that the serious incident that hurt you was not a fatal incident that killed you. It's because of your covering that you stood strong in the middle of the very things that broke others to pieces. It's because of your covering that you remain destined for greatness despite the difficulties you face. Praise God for covering! Shout about covering! Rejoice with a good reason! After all, your Lord cared enough to place your life *"among the reeds."*

Notes *and* Personal Reflections: My Head vs. My Heart

TEN

WATCHED

"The baby's sister then stood at a distance, watching to see what would happen to him."
Exodus 2:4 NLT

Perhaps there is nothing more unsettling than the feelings of loneliness and helplessness—especially during the times we must make tough decisions and take some actions that really cut us to the core. These seasons in our lives can certainly take their toll us on physically, mentally, emotionally, and spiritually. However, it's important to know that the *feeling* of loneliness is not indicative that we are actually alone. There is nothing we can do, nothing we can face, nothing we can endure, nothing we can cry or lament over, and nothing that affects us that our Father in heaven is not keenly aware of. The whole premise of this chapter rests on this one principle: no matter where life leads us there is no need to worry because we're always watched!

Jochebed finally did it. She prepared Moses' personal boat, placed it in the reeds, and let him go. Yet, while the little baby floated in the Nile by himself, he was not alone. His sister, Miriam, stood by and kept the basket containing Moses in her sight. Miriam couldn't and wouldn't be content on just letting Moses float away. The love she had for her brother and her family wouldn't allow it. The relationship she'd developed—if only for three months—with her

Decisions

brother created the necessity within Miriam to keep a watchful eye on Moses. Can I take a moment to suggest something to you regarding those who compose your crowd, your inner circle? Only embark upon and embrace relationships in which there is mutual feeling of necessity to always keep watch over one another. It really doesn't matter the nature of the relationship—just friends, romantically involved, family members, Church FAMILY, parent and children, and etc.—those people who invoke intimate feelings from you should at least care enough to never let you endure some of life's most crucial moments alone. Conversely, you should care about them enough to never allow them to live life alone. We should personify Miriam and be close enough to "watch" our friends and loved ones during the good times, the bad times, the highs, the lows, the times of laughter, and the times of tears. However, as well see in a moment, watching doesn't yield complacency. Instead, it creates a willingness to step up in a moment's notice to make the difference in someone's life (again, we'll see this shortly by taking note of Miriam's actions).

I remember when our youngest daughter, Emani, was born. Shortly after what appeared to be a normal birth, she began to have, among a myriad of things, some serious respiratory problems. The little thing could hardly breathe. Truth is, the first several hours of her life, my faith was really weakened and I had come to grips, as best as I could, that she may leave us only a few hours after coming into the world. Praise be to God that, very slowly, but surely, things began to improve. Still Emani was placed in the hospital's Neonatal Intensive Care Unit.

Decisions

Several times a day for many days we visited Emani. I'll never forget one day our son Kaleb, my mother, and I went into the NICU to visit Emani. She was crying something fierce (which actually was a good thing because her crying was indicative that she was getting stronger...man I felt something with that). When we got over to the little incubator in which Emani was kept, the most heartfelt thing happened. After watching his baby sister for a few minutes and listening to her cry, Kaleb opened the door on the side of the incubator, placed in hand on her little back and said, *"Don't worry Emani! It's okay. You're big brother is here now!"* Almost immediately she calmed down and stopped crying. Her brother let her know she wasn't alone. Kaleb let her know that he had been watching her. Kaleb let his little sister know that he was right there with her. Likewise, it's quite possible that you're facing some of the most unimaginable situations in your life. If not, as sure as you live difficulties will come at some point or another. In life there will be days for all us that we'll be like Emani and getting into our "little incubator" and just cry and cry and cry. Life will always present seasons when it seems a little bit of everything is wrong. Still there is great news! You have a Big Brother—Jesus Christ our Lord—who is watching every single thing concerning you. The Bible says that when it comes to our Lord, not even a sparrow falls without the Father noticing (Matthew 10:29). That's to say even the little sparrow is so important to God that He values it and keeps His eye on it. In the same manner, we can celebrate and be comforted because our Lord's eyes are always upon us. When we take this fact to heart, we should be able to hear His voice saying, "*<u>Your name</u> ! Don't worry! It's okay!*

Decisions

I'm here!" Isn't it good news that no matter what comes our way we can be comforted and walk in faith because we're always on Heaven's surveillance?

Notes *and* Personal Reflections: My Head vs. My Heart

ELEVEN

RESCUED

"Soon after this, one of Pharaoh's daughters came down to bathe in the river, and her servant girls walked along the riverbank. When the princess saw the little basket among the reeds, she told one of her servant girls to get it for her. As the princess opened it, she found the baby boy. His helpless cries touched her heart. 'He must be one of the Hebrew children,'" she said.
Exodus 2:5-6 NLT

It's unfortunate, but we've all witnessed the tragedies and disasters in which rescue personnel are called in to look for people possibly affected by what had happened. A phrase we're likely familiar with is "Search and Rescue." When the firefighters, rescue squads, police officers, military personnel, and others use this term, it lights a flame of hope. You see, as long as it's a search and rescue effort there is reason to believe that there are people who have survived the tragedy. Yes, they may be bruised; but they survived. They may be wounded; but they survived. They may have injuries that will require a long time before total healing takes place; but they survived. The great news is that in many search and rescue cases, there are survivors. The news that is even better is that there are those who care enough to expend time, energy, effort, and resources to look for survivors, to reach out to them, nurture

Decisions

them, assess their needs, and then get them to the help they so desperately need.

This is exactly what happened to Baby Moses. He was in his personal little boat when Pharaoh's daughter and her servant girls discovered his basket floating in the Nile. No, they didn't set out from home searching for Moses. In fact, finding a baby wasn't on their day's agenda. The princess and her servant girls had simply gone to the river to bathe. Who could've possibly known that a rescue mission was about to take place? Let me pause here for a moment and express to you what I tell the members of the New Life Church all of the time. When a person is intimate with God and enjoys a true, nurturing, love relationship with Him, things don't "just happen." There is no such thing as coincidence. Everything good that takes place is the result of God's awesome master plan unfolding. You didn't "just so happen" to see someone that you haven't seen in a while, and they really encouraged you. God orchestrated it so your paths would cross. You didn't "by chance" meet the love of your life at the event you weren't really excited about attending. God made sure the time and place matched so you would meet. It's not just a coincidence that you shared with a friend your frustrations about some medical ailments you've been quietly dealing with for quite a while with no relief and in turn they recommended you to a physician that had helped them with the same issue. God has a way of working things together (Romans 8:28) in His own timing and way. I'll never forget Sunday, January 23, 2000. That's a day that changed my life. We were having an afternoon worship service at my home Church. We had a guest church coming in to lead the worship that

Decisions

day. I had a friend who belonged to the guest church. She called and said she was coming to the worship and was bringing a friend with her. I thought absolutely nothing of it. It "so happened" (yeah, I know...LOL) my friend and I arrived at the Church at the same time. As I got out of my car, the friend of my friend was getting out of my friend's car as well. The moment I laid eyes on her I was uniquely intrigued. She was beautiful. She was classy. She was elegant. She was confident; yet she had this gentle, humble disposition. Yes, I discerned all of this in a good thirty seconds! Well, as I'm writing at this moment the friend of a friend has been my wife for more than twelve years. You get my point? The worship service, the specific guest church that was to lead the worship, my friend belonging to that church, my friend bringing her friend that day, the meeting, the marrying, the merging, and now the three kids were all a part of God's plan orchestrated for my life and for Felicia's life. It wasn't coincidence; but destiny. It was not happenstance; but HIM!

Likewise, it was God's plan that Pharaoh's daughter took a bath at time she did and at the particular place along the river that she did. If the Master had not orchestrated it, the princess wouldn't have been in place at the right time to even notice the basket containing Moses. What an awesome God we serve! The princess noticed the basket and had her servants to bring the basket to her. To her surprise, when she opened the basket there was Moses. She recognized Moses as one of the Hebrew children. Yet, the text says that *"his helpless cries touched her heart."* Remember, it was the princess' father—Pharaoh—that had ordered that all newborn Israelite males be thrown into the Nile. It was

Decisions

her father who had earlier decreed that all Israelite males be killed. So it is logical to think that when the princess saw this Hebrew baby that she would've just obeyed her father and killed him. Not so! Moses cried out and his cries touched the princess' heart to effect that she was drawn to him with compassion and care.

Moses' cry made the difference! It's something about seeing and hearing a child cry that touches the heart of most people. In the same sense that Moses' cry led to his rescue, our cries before our Heavenly Father will lead to our rescue as well. Our daughter Emani loves school. However, the fine people at First Missionary Baptist Church Child Development Center and Academy know very well that Emani's love for school developed in "later years." My gosh! For the first couple of years it took a couple of months for her to get acclimated each time a new school session began. Every, single day it was the same routine. The moment we pulled up at school her eyes swelled with tears, the tears would begin to fall, and the closer we got to the front door the worse it got. However, all things considered, Emani would hold it together pretty good until it was time for her to go into the room with the other kids. Then she cut loose! Wailing. Crying. Having a fit! Eventually she got to the point that she held it together pretty good until I got out of sight. However, before I could get to the outer doors of the building the crying, hollering, and screaming began. The funny thing is that Emani was by no means the only child who cried. Often there were three or four or more kids who cried at the same time as well. However, no matter how many kids were opening their mouths wide and letting their displeasure with being at school rip, I could

Decisions

always tell which voice was Emani's. I'm her father. She's my child. I'm specially tuned into the voice of my child. I know the voice. I know the shrill. I know the intensity that she cries with. Many times it was too much for me to bear. I knew Emani was safe. I knew she was in the hands of people who cared for her. I knew eventually she'd calm down. However, there were times that her cry arrested my heart, caused me to turn around, and go back to "rescue" her for a few minutes. I needed to touch her. I needed to hug her. I needed her to know that Daddy understood and that things would be okay (mmmmm..that's how I felt MOST of the time...LOL). Perhaps you're reading this now and your situation has you feeling like Emani. You're uncomfortable. You're feeling left and alone. You're unsettled. You're hurt. You're disappointed. You're fretting a bit about the unknown. Well, let me encourage you! Your rescue is not far away. However, you've got to cry out. You've got to be real and transparent about how you feel. You've got to be honest about the state of your heart, mind, and spirit. Cry out to God. Cry out to your Father. Just like the kids at Emani's school, many other people our crying out God too. However, you must know that you Father is specially tuned to your cry. He feels your pain. He's affected by your anguish. He wants nothing more than to "hug" you and make very plain to you that He's there for you. He understands your pain. He's never going to leave you in the midst of whatever it is that is causing you to cry. He's ready to rescue you. You have purpose. He has plans for your life. That's why He's especially faithful to hear your cry. The older saints used to sing an old metered hymn that says, *"I love the Lord. He heard my cry and pitied every groan. As long as I live and trouble rises, I'll hasten to His throne."*

Friend, cry and see won't He come to the rescue!

Notes *and* Personal Reflections: My Head vs. My Heart

TWELVE

IT WAS A DIVINE SET-UP

"The baby's sister approached the princess. 'Should I go and find one of the Hebrew women to nurse the baby for you?' she asked. 'Yes, do!' the princess replied. So the girl rushed home and called the baby's mother." **Exodus 2:7-8 NLT**

Often, one of the hardest things to do is to find any good coming out of bad situations. At least initially, it's not a faith issue at all. We're humans. When things go wrong it's simply natural to have some natural moments. Hurt is real. Tears really do fall. Disappointment is not some illusion. Pain, be it physical, emotional, or spiritual, is not some abstract thing. Being devastated is often the real, expected response when tragic things happen. A temporary feeling of helplessness and even hopelessness is palpable when it seems that life has suddenly shot downward in a spiral and there's absolutely nothing you can do to stop the madness. However, there is one thing we can take to the bank. For people of faith, God has a way of using our setbacks as set-ups for something greater than we can imagine. Our Master has a unique way of taking trouble and turning it around in such a way that all we can do is scream, *"Look at God!"*

That's probably how Jochebed had to have felt when God's providence flipped the script regarding Moses. It's not biblically read, but I think it's very safe to assume that

Decisions

Jochebed's heart was broken and tears flowed after she released her son into the Nile River in his custom-made basket. Never mind that it was for his own good. It still hurt. Never mind that in his mother's mind, it was likely Moses' only true hope of survival. This was still her baby boy that she placed among the reeds. It's certainly not beyond reason to think that Jochebed felt a myriad of emotions—pain, hurt, inadequacy because she couldn't truly protect her son, fear, and so much more. BUT GOD! He turned things around. All that Jochebed had been through and felt was simply a divine set-up that only God could orchestrate. Remember from Chapter 10 that Moses' sister Miriam stood and watched the basket after their mom placed it in the river. She kept an eye on her brother and all that would transpire with him. If we kind of log what happens from there, it's easy to see the divine set-up. Watch this unfold. Jochebed puts Moses' basket in the river. Miriam watches Moses' basket as it sits in the reeds. Miriam sees when the princess and her servants come to the river to bathe. The princess sees the basket in the reeds. The servants bring the basket to Pharaoh's daughter. She opens the basket and baby Moses is crying. The princess recognizes Moses as one of the Hebrew children. According to her father's decree, she was supposed to kill Moses by throwing him into the river to drown—BUT she doesn't. Moses' cries touch the princess' heart. Miriam is still around and walks—unannounced—over to the princess and offers a suggestion to "go find" a Hebrew mother to nurse Moses. The princess agrees. Miriam goes home and finds the perfect person to nurse Moses—JOCHEBED! *Look at God!* Who else could've orchestrated such a feat in which

Decisions

Jochebed releases Moses into uncertainty and then turns right around and receives him again with the "job" to do what she's done all and along and a "job" any godly mother would want—to love and nurture her baby. From the get-go, the situation with Moses was a set-up to favor Moses by saving his life. After all, as we know God had big plans for him. It was a set up to favor Jochebed by giving her son back to her. It was a set up for Miriam by allowing to her to be in the right place at the right time so that God could orchestrate the family reunion through her. Friend, God has a way of turning trouble to triumph. God has a way of turning sadness and sorry into celebration. Our faith must believe that no matter how things look, things are going to get better.

Yes, I know! That's easy preaching, but he harder living! I get it. I often experience it. It's hard to see the good in the lay-off. It's hard to see the good in the cutback of hours at work when you need every, single dime you can muster. It's hard to fathom something good coming out of the accident. It's hard to see the sunshine after a longtime relationship finally ends. However, we must know that Romans 8:28 really is true. God has a unique way in which He can use every life situation as pieces to a master puzzle and position them in such a way that we're better and blessed no matter what. Sometimes, it's hard for us to grasp this concept. This is especially true in the midst of troubling times. Sometimes it may take hours, days, weeks, months, or even years for us to see the greater things that God had in store all along. In all of these scenarios, we as believers must trust God IN all things and FOR all things. We must stand on His promises and His Word even when

Decisions

we don't understand Him. We have to continue to believe that even the most unpleasant, hurtful, and sometimes unexpected situations are set-ups to *make* us better. They are set-ups to *bring* us better. Most of all, they are set-ups to ensure that God gets the glory for the great things He does.

On Thursday, June 5, 2014 our home took a direct hit from lightning. There was moderate damage on the outside. However, just about everything electrical on the inside was fried. All of the televisions, the computers, the kitchen appliances, the garage door motor, the telephone and internet equipment, the home security system, the doorbell, and many electrical outlets were toast. It was a scary, frustrating, and tedious situation. We had no ability to refrigerate anything. We had no ability to cook anything. No televisions to watch. Even if the televisions had survived, we had no satellite service because it was destroyed too. I mean, it was crazy. For a little more than day, I was having my humanly, fleshly moments. I wasn't happy. I "think" I might have even said a fleshly word or two (pray for me....smh). In fact, I was a bit angry. We had lost a lot. However, I couldn't and didn't sulk long. After all, nothing would change with me having a pity party-tantrum continually. So the first thing I did was to think about what had happened. Yes, we had lost quite a bit. However, the house didn't have extensive damage and was still standing. We still had our clothes and other possessions. We were still alive! All of these things were reasons to give God thanks even in difficult situations. I was also grateful that we have great insurance. Therefore, everything would be replaced. Suddenly, when the new appliances and the new televisions and

Decisions

etc. starting coming in, I realized that the lightning strike was just a set-up. Once the claims were settled, we ended up with bigger and better stuff. In the end, just about everything that we got to replace what we'd lost was a significant upgrade. You see the point here, my friend? No, the lightning strike was not planned; neither was it fun. No, all of the paperwork and running here and there was not fun. No, the days and nights my family was displaced was not enjoyable. Even the shopping and comparing prices for new items became tiring and tedious. However, in the end we have "greater" after going through a troubling ordeal.

Friend, I don't know what you've endured or are currently going through. I know that it's really hard to see the good things through the bad. However, by faith begin singing to yourself the lyrics to a popular song by Gospel artist

Dorothy Norwood, *"The storm is almost gone. The storm is almost gone. I can see the sun peeking through the clouds. The storm is almost gone."*

Notes *and* Personal Reflections: My Head vs. My Heart

THIRTEEN

JUST DO WHAT YOU DO

"'Take this child home and nurse him for me,' the princess told her. 'I will pay you for your help.' So the baby's mother took her baby home and nursed him." **Exodus 2:9 NLT**

Perhaps you've heard the old saying, *"I love it when a plan comes together."* There is no greater feeling to see and experience things work out like or even better than you've planned. Furthermore, nothing compares to that feeling we get when God's set-up ultimately plays out and is spotlighted in our lives. In the same manner that we can only imagine the pain and hurt that Jochebed must have felt when placing her baby Moses in the Nile River, we can only imagine the elation and jubilance she experienced when God made a way for her baby to come back to her arms. When Miriam went back to find a "Hebrew woman" to nurse the baby that Pharaoh's daughter had just found, can you imagine the utter amazement that must have come to Jochebed's mind when she was told she was about to get her baby back? I'm sure Jochebed was full of joy and unbelief that same time. I'm sure she asked Miriam was she sure of what she was saying. She may have even told her daughter to stop playing and toying with her emotions. However, it was really about to happen. Baby Moses was coming home! Not only that, Jochebed was about to blessed for simply being who she was—Moses' mom!

Decisions

The text says that when Jochebed came before the princess, the princess basically told her, "Ma'am, thank you for coming! I have a little Hebrew boy here that needs nursing. I'd like for you to take him home and nurse him for me. I know I may be asking a lot; but if you nurse him I'll pay you well." Man, I LOVE IT when a plan—God's plan—comes together! Jochebed is about to paid to be who she was—a mother. She was about to get paid to do what she'd done for the three months prior to this moment—nurse and nurture her baby! Look at this. Making the bold decision led Jochebed to a place of blessings. Making the difficult decision positioned her in a place of prosperity. Making the impossible decision placed her in a place of improbable favor! No one could work this out like our God. It's almost like God said to Jochebed and says to us, "Just do I as lead you and do the things I've blessed you to do best and you'll see work on your behalf!"

Friend, as I prepare to close this writing, I want to encourage you to just do what you do. You are uniquely made. You are uniquely gifted. You are uniquely positioned for great things. No one IS you. No can BE you. Furthermore, you'll never be a better someone else than you can be as yourself. Jochebed teaches us that our place of blessing and unusual favor is tucked deeply in the fabric of each us being true to who we are. Again, Jochebed was paid to do what she'd done all along and to be who she'd been all along. Being Moses' mother—the best mother she could be—was the exact place that she found God orchestrating blessings for her.

You know, I'm not T.D Jakes, Joel Osteen, Bishop Joseph W. Walker III or any other world-renowned preacher and pastor. However, I am

Decisions

Antoyne L. Green. I had to come to the realization that I don't have to be famous to be uniquely gifted. There is a certain anointing and there are certain gifts, certain talents, certain methods, and etc. that are indigenous to me and me alone. To be blessed materially, emotionally, financially, and spiritually I've learned that no matter what life presents, just be me. I've learned that no matter how hard the decisions are that I must make, make them with the help of God and do as Jochebed did and "stay close" while God works things out. It's then I'll experience the exponential blessings ranging from finances to simple peace because there is favor and blessing upon being the genuine Antoyne L. Green. It's the same thing for you my friend. If you're a preacher, no one can preach like you're uniquely gifted to preach. If you're a teacher or singer, no one else has that "special it" that was grafted into you. No one can be "Dad" or "Mom" to your kids like you can. No one else can encourage others with the gift of encouragement like you have. You get it, friend! This list can go on and on. However, the message is the same in any analogy here. The blessings are found in "you doing you" in the unique way God designed.

Finally, Jochebed's tough decision turned out well fairly quickly. Balance in this presentation allows me to hope the same for you; but also mandates me to inform you that your turnaround may not be instantly. I also must tell you that often one tough decision is often followed by another one. After Moses was older, verse 10 says *"the child's mother brought him back to the princess, who adopted him as her son. The princess name him Moses, for she said, 'I drew him out of the water.'"* Yes,

Decisions

Jochebed released her son again. So another hard decision had to be made. However, her release of him led to him being one of God's best leaders, heralds, and examples. By no means was Moses perfect, but we know from history he was a major part of God's plan. However, none of this could've happened without Jochebed making the tough decisions. The key in all decision-making is to first be willing to do the right thing regardless. Then we must allow God to speak to us—even when we don't want to hear it or if we're not comfortable with His directions—so we'll know exactly what's the right thing to do. Then we must ask Him for boldness to make the decisions He's led us to. Finally, we must trust Him that He's working things out for our good, others' good, and for His glory. In meantime, while we wait for all things to work out, we must remain faith-filled and patient. Even in tears, pain, disappointment, anxiety, and other emotional seasons, we must hold the hope that God's up to something for our good. Eventually peace will come until God's providence is realized.

> ALSO BY
>
> ANTOYNE L. GREEN

However God Chooses
He May Not Do It Your Way

You pray. You have faith that God will answer your prayers in specific way. Then God answers your prayers. However, He does things differently than you asked and anticipated. So how are we to handle it when it God's plan for our lives conflicts with our plan for our lives? What do we do when God doesn't do what we want, when we want, and how we want? In this book, the Old Testament character Naaman will teach us both the wrong way and the right way to handle it when God doesn't do things our way. It's very likely that you'll find yourself on the front seat of Naaman's emotional roller coaster. It's probable that as you read Naaman's words that you'll hear your own voice as you recall certain situations in your life. Read this book and assume the position of a student and consider Naaman as your teacher. You'll learn valuable insights into walking by faith as God moves in your life however He chooses.

www.ingramcontent.com/pod-product-compliance
Lightning Source LLC
Chambersburg PA
CBHW061650040426
42446CB00010B/1678